King's Applause

"The brilliant new book ... Dr. Angelise M. Rouse is an indispensable ... young African-American males to reach their highest potential in all important facets of life. The book astutely addresses all of the salient points that young African-American males need to properly define his identity, develop his intellect, and position themselves for greatness despite any social, economic, political, or spiritual obstacles that society might impose. It is imperative that young African-American males properly equip themselves with a full armor to be successful in mainstream society and not live beneath their natural and spiritual privilege.

Our young men are ordained to be leaders and not followers and take their rightful place in academia, government, the private sector, their communities, and most importantly in their homes. The potential of the collective intellectual capital resident in the minds of young African-American males can unleash innovative breakthroughs impacting this nation and the world at large.

Every young African-American male who carefully reads and applies the life transforming principles contained in **The King Inside** will position himself on a trajectory for continual success and self-mastery. The American educational community should take note of this important book and incorporate it into their leadership development curriculums. If adopted, we'll see higher levels of academic and professional achievement amongst young African-American males and lower levels of young African-American males entrapped in the penal system, engaged in destructive social behavior, and feeling a sense of helplessness and marginalization.

There is a sense of urgency for all young African-American males to consistently raise the performance bar and set a higher standard for their peers. Dr. Angelise M. Rouse's book communicates that sense of urgency and clearly articulates practical principles easily applied by our young African-American males to make the ontological transformation into true manhood.

My recommendation to all conscientious African-Americans is to continue to fervently pray for our young men and to purchase as many copies of **The King Inside** and distribute them to all young African-American males within their sphere of influence."

Dr. Frederick R. Lester,
Global Managing Director
Men's Empowerment Network

*"**The King Inside** lays the groundwork for our young African-American males as they navigate their way through life and the societies they inhabit. Dr. Rouse demonstrates that with hard work and a strong support system, our young black men can become successful regardless of their race, class, and social circumstances. She makes important points when discussing black males within the educational system, and how the value of education is worth reiterating beyond High School. **The King Inside** is a must read and a wonderful guide for people of all ages!"*

Evan Burnett
Youth Counselor,
Rochester City School District

"If the foundations are destroyed, what can the righteous do?" -Psalm 11:3.

Foundations determine everything. There's too many useless attempts at living life and not enough of building a life right for living. In **The King Inside: Practical Advice for Young African-American Males**, Dr. Angelise Rouse challenges our young men to not leave "home" without the fundamentals. Schools are supposed to prepare you academically. Life skills are not high on the list of priorities. This practical tool is a clear guide, that can be in itself a "type" of mentor that will instruct, direct, and position each young man who applies the wisdom and advice written in it for success in life."

Wilbur Brown
Special Educator, Seminar Presenter
Maryland School District

"From family to citizenry, practicality and self-efficacy is the message of **The King Inside**; and here-in lies the societal challenge - helping adolescent males of color reach their full potential. Dr. Rouse has established with this book a simplistic yet worthy premise for helping adolescents, young men of color see and be success."

R. Bey Muhammad
Multicultural Studies Instructor
Central Piedmont Community College

"Dr. Rouse's newest work, **The King Inside: Practical Advice for Young African-American Males**, is not just another book to be added to the library shelves of theories about the African-American experience. Instead, it's an invaluable guide for African-American youth, and an indispensable tool for teachers, parents, and other leaders who want to influence them in positive directions. Filled with practical wisdom and powerful principles, this outstanding work can quickly become a difference maker in the lives of countless students who need help in navigating the shoals of adversity to reach the shores of opportunity."

Rev. Brian Vieira
Founder and President
ScholarSkills Inc.

"In my career as a corrections officer, I've worked with boys and young Black men with serious behavioral issues. In time, I came to realize that an overwhelming number of these young men had no real clue of who they were or a sense of self. I've had countless conversations with them and soon came to realize that the absence of a father and positive male role model severely affected their ability to make good decisions and to navigate through basic everyday responsibilities. **The King Inside** addresses these issues and provides a clear blueprint for young men to follow and guide them into manhood. Dr. Rouse has put together the basic essentials towards young adulthood and staying on the right track. She reinforces what it takes to stay on top in a society built to see them fail. It is a must read for young Black men!"

Terence Ware
State Corrections

"The King Inside is a very powerful and practical book for young men today. Young men need to understand how to reach their true value and potential. The foundation of anything is crucial for its survival and success. This book highlights the foundations which are vital to growth and success. It is filled with applicable principles needed for young men today. The quotes in this book are on point. I recommend this book for young men who are in need of motivation to reach their highest potential."

Eliud Sicard
Youth Minister
Motivational Speaker
Community Activist, Chicago, IL

"The King Inside: Practical Advice for Young African-American Males is a dynamic book outlining a viable path to help young African-American males become successful in a world highly influenced by distractions. Dr. Rouse's approach is practical in the sense that it establishes a realistic framework to navigate the challenges young African-American males will face enroute to manhood. The topics in the book speak to the totality of the human persona and addresses foundations that fuel balance in a young man's relationship with others. Every obstacle one will face in life can be conquered through certain skill-sets: preparation, planning, determination, and persistence. **The King Inside** emphasizes the importance of executing those skill-sets, which collectively produces a diverse individual who conquers life in every realm (i.e. education, family/social relationships, financial, self-reliance, etc.).

Ananias Williams III,
Senior IT Executive

"Great work! Wonderful ideas! This book offers young African-American males great insights into the realities of some of the challenges they may find after they leave the folds of high school. It is a wonderful transition tool! It is also a great resource for educators who may benefit from analyzing the experiences of students who come from diverse and sometimes very challenging situations. It opens educators' eyes in acknowledging how to best encourage young men with reasonable approaches to solving problems and pointing them to the resources that would benefit them. **The King Inside** gives the reader a gentle, but real reminder of how to engage in positive approaches to achieve success by learning to identify a wide range of role models who have clear and successful career paths. This book is certainly a powerful tool that will help to bring out the best in our young African-American males helping them to realize their worth as true champions and kings of an evolving generation."

Edris Ryan, Ph.D
Inclusion Specialist, Special Educator
Licensed Exceptional Children
Program Administrator
Member of Council of Exceptional Children, USA
www.proaccessedu.com

"Dr. Rouse has written a riveting piece of work catered to exposing practical advice for maturing young men. This body of work proposes great examples engrossed by real life enlightenment. She has arranged fundamental data for young adults transitioning from High School to Adulthood via College or Work Professional; even providing a prerequisite for finding a mentor. Every young African-American male should read this book. "Think of education as a personal investment in yourself."

Rev. Derrell Young
Young Adult Minister
RELEVANT, Charlotte, NC

THE
KING
INSIDE

Practical Advice for Young African-American Males

Dr. Angelise M. Rouse

Printed in the United States of America

2016 First Edition

10 9 8 7 6 5 4 3 2 1

Subject Index:

Rouse, Angelise M.

Title: The King Inside: Practical Advice for Young African-American Males

1. Black   2. Youth   3. Empowerment   4. Inspirational

5. Self-Help

Paperback ISBN: 978-0-9976546-0-8

Ebook ISBN: 978-0-9976546-1-5

Author Photo Credit: Chase Photography

www.chasephotography.org

Especially 4 Me Publishing LLC

especially4mepublishing.com

drangeliserouse.com

www.especially4mepublishing.com

Also published by Dr. Rouse

Especially 4 Me

A Student's Guide To Understanding The IEP

Angelise M. Rouse, Ph.D.

*This book is dedicated to my parents,
Lloyd and Dorothy Rouse.*

Acknowledgements

There have been so many individuals who have contributed to my personal growth and development, and they are too many to name, yet you know who you are. I would like to express my gratitude to the many people who saw me through this book. To all those who provided support, talked things over, reviewed, offered comments, allowed me to quote their remarks, thank you.

I would like to thank my mom, Dorothy Rouse, whose influence on my life is far too great to capture on a single page. The older I get, the more I see our similarities. I only hope that one day I will be a Godly influence on my children and leave a legacy, just like her. Thank you, mom, for all that you have done for me so graciously and sacrificially. To my dad, Lloyd Rouse, who passed away in June of 2013 due to complications from a stroke. There were no warnings, no time for goodbyes. My dad, although quiet, was a great man with impeccable character. He was hard-working and an exemplary model of a Christian man. I will never forget the dozens of spiritual conversations around that crowded dinner table on Sylvan Lane. No matter who came over (or who we visited), it seemed the conversation always ended up about Christ. Thank you dad for being the most influential man in my life.

To my one and only sister, Anita and her husband Terence. My brothers Calvin and his wife Lisa, James and David. To all my nieces and nephews, my three wonderful children, Terrell Sr., Aaron, Alyse and grandson, Terrell Jr., who provide unending inspiration. To my colleagues, friends and social media acquaintances, I am very appreciative of your encouragement, support and acts of kindness. Last, but certainly not least, my editor, Kim Rouse, thank you for helping me bring this project to fruition.

A Message to Young Males...

You are a king from the day you were created. You do not have to conform to the current stereotypes and images placed over you from the social media and the politically motivated news on television. Never hold your head down and give the oppressor any advantage to come for you. What matters is not where you come from, but what plans you have for your future. I easily could've been a statistic, but I learned that you must **P.U.S.H. = Persevere Under Strong Hardships!** This too shall pass. The same people who scandalize your name one day may eventually need your help in this cruel world. Be better. Do better. Strive! Conquer!

LaMarcus J. Hall, M Ed.
Doctoral Student at Purdue University
Curriculum and Instruction Program

Contents

INTRODUCTION

*"The ultimate expression of generosity
is not in giving of what you have,
but in giving of who you are."*

— Johnnetta B. Cole

The King Inside stems from a deeply rooted passion to empower today's young African-American males with a practical game plan to guide them from adolescence through manhood. The success rate for the statics of young men comprising this demographic are utterly frightening. Whether we look at literacy, high school dropout, incarceration, repeat offenders, or death, the sheer volume of this "counted-out" group, should send shocks to the system of any adult human being, regardless of race, creed, or ethnicity.

Our heritage is filled with a rich history of African-American kings and queens. We can look to documented successful people in every facet of life: scientists, inventors, doctors, entrepreneurs, and the list goes on. Why are our young men failing? Why have they lost hope? What actions can we take as a community, as parents, as teachers and ordinary citizens? What actions can *they* take to better themselves?

A central focus of my work involves promoting the academic achievement of youth in urban schools by addressing Special Education Reform. My target focus is on the enormous number of public school classrooms that are composed of nearly 100% minority males. I have published research and scholarly articles and editorials on Special Education Policy, student achievement, youth violence, and race and ethnic relations in America. In addition, I have conducted qualitative research on the overrepresentation of African-American males systematically greenlighted into special education programs, despite the flashing red signals that it is a terrible misdiagnosis.

As the mother of two adult sons, six nephews, and being a Special Education professional for over a decade, I am committed to doing my part in helping to eradicate the dismal negative statistics. The impetus of this project stemmed from my dissertation research on the subject, as well as my oldest son Terrell's favorite movie, *Disney's The Lion King*. I believe he and I watched this movie more than 100 times during his childhood. For some reason, King Mufasa's powerful message to his son Simba, the young prince, that there was a king inside of him resonated with me then, and still does today. Our young men must realize that it is in fact a "jungle" out there, but they have the tools within themselves to control their destiny. It is time for them to take their rightful place on the throne in their respective kingdoms.

My objective is to motivate these young men with knowledge to succeed while navigating life's challenges. This is not a project to elaborate on the negative aspects affecting this group in our communities. There is enough written about it by talented individuals who have worked with and studied this issue their entire careers. More importantly, there is plenty of hate, division, and negativity disproportionately targeted at young African-American males daily, and not enough general life-knowledge that is common to us as adults. No one book can cover everything, however, I hope that **The King Inside**, strikes a chord with this demographic to help them become productive citizens, and accomplish their dreams and goals. It's the least I can do!

Dr. Angelise M. Rouse
July 2016
Burlington, NJ

*"You have forgotten who you are...
Look inside yourself,
you are more than what
you have become..."*

Mufasa, The Lion King

King

The literal meaning of a king is a sole male ruler; a monarch, usually inheriting the throne as a birthright. As you know, we do not have this type of governing structure in the U.S. However, references to "King" in this book are used as a metaphor to demonstrate the necessity of you taking charge of your future. Your king-like leadership should be evident and unleashed over yourself, other people, and situations. You are never too young to accept responsibility and be accountable for your actions. Man up to your kingship role!

Foundation

The word Foundation is used throughout this book. It is the base of something; the underlying structure of a thing. Without a strong foundation buildings and other structures would collapse. Similarly, if you don't have a strong foundation in the ten general life skills provided in this book, you will miss out on the core fundamental skills needed to succeed in life. **The King Inside** aims to give you the practical foundation you need as you walk into manhood.

App #1

Family Foundation

*"In every conceivable manner, the family
is the link to our past, bridge to our future."*

— *Alex Haley*

Life is about choices. Yet despite all of the choices you will make in life, you don't get to choose your family. Each person in your household or those closely extended outside of your home, were placed in your life for a specific purpose. The family structure was created so that everyone (even your parents) could have some understanding of order and authority over our lives. In other words, we all must be accountable to someone. As children, everything we learn about relationships comes from our families. Whether our blood family, through marriage, adoption, foster or extended family.

Now that you are a young man, you may think that your family is not important. You are at an age seeking independence from your parents and other adults whom you feel just don't get where you're coming from. In reality, that thought process couldn't be further from the truth. More than likely, your parents and extended family have gone through similar or worse circumstances when they were teens. The key is that they have survived and can offer you advice and real-life examples of how to handle them. Don't shut them out. Honor and respect your parents and elders. They are critical to your personal growth and development.

By the same token, there is a certain level of regard

that must be shown to your peers. It's OK if you don't get along with a sibling, cousin or other relative. We are all unique and have different personalities. Everyone is not going to get along with each other *all* the time. However, the key is to tolerate and respect each other's differences. The truth of the matter is, as you mature, and embark upon your own relationships, you will learn how to handle various personalities and situations with a different perspective. Over time, you will see that your parents, siblings, cousins, and classmates are not so bad after all. Learning to control your anger and attitude, by putting forth an effort to get along with others, is also an important skill to acquire.

Even if you are from a single-parent home, don't use that as an excuse for any area where you are lacking. There are tons of resources in your community, schools, and religious organizations, to help fill the void that you need from a male parent. Use your situation to empower you to work harder, instead of justification to do little or nothing to advance your future. As a single mother, I have been fortunate to have my father, brothers, and brother-in-law fill the gap for an absent father in my household to help raise my two sons. I am truly grateful for their efforts because I see the impact they have had in the lives of my sons.

In many urban schools, there is a large population of homeless male students. I have heard several horror stories of group homes and foster care settings. Don't let one experience stop you from finding shelter. If you have left an unsafe environment, yet are continuing to come to school, I urge you to reach out to a counselor to help place you in alternate or temporary housing with the state or community organization. There are other social workers and teams of people who are there to provide you with the necessities to live.

King's Wisdom...

"Be open to advice. Even if you think that it doesn't apply, listen. It may not apply now, but it may save your life later."

—Musa Abdullah, MSW
Behavioral Specialist

Without a strong team of individuals who genuinely have your best interest at heart, you are bound to waste time and prolong your destiny. The clock will continue to tick whether you get your priorities straight now or later. Seek out more one-on-one time with your parents and older adults to ask questions and share situations that you are struggling with. It's really OK to ask for help.

Foster Family

Having the support of family and loved ones is a great boost to your overall success. A large majority of the male students in my classes were part of a state foster system. Being in a foster system is tough, but with a positive mindset to better yourself, you can tear down the stereotypes and achieve your dreams. Family does not have to be blood. Family is the person or persons who love and care for you. Like with any family situation, there will be good times and bad. Try your best to handle the bad with respect and maturity. Reach out to your school counselor or your social worker to help you handle family or home issues.

Yes, being in foster care may appear like the worst thing that could ever happen to you. But, no matter the outcome, you will be faced with adulthood and there can be no more excuses for not giving your best. There are several well-known people who are products of a foster system, as well as thousands of extraordinary people who are leading fulfilling lives. People like the late Steve Jobs who invented your iPhone, iPad, iPod, comedian Tommy Davidson, Actor and Rapper Ice-T, and several players in the NFL and NBA were in foster care early in their lives.

We don't get to choose our family, but we get to

choose how we adapt and function in the family that we are given.

RULES

Of course you probably hate the current rules of your household. That's normal. Rules are necessary learning tools for your future. I'm not saying that every rule makes sense or is even fair. Yet the sooner you realize that you cannot do whatever you want to do because you are "grown," the less consequences you will have to face as you get older.

Rules don't disappear when you move out of your parent's house. Yes, you should still clean your room or apartment and pick up after yourself. That's a personal hygiene issue and choice that you will have to deal with on your own. However, keep in mind that whatever educational or work environment that becomes your next step once you leave home, will have more rules than you ever imagined.

For example, all schools (high schools, colleges and universities) have some type of student handbook which outlines the school code of conduct and actually lists all of the things that you can and cannot do. You are actually given the handbook to review and sign, indicating that you understand and agree to the rules. These handbooks are usually 20 pages or more! That's definitely a lot more rules than you had at home. Violation of several student handbook rules will lead to you being kicked out—point blank. So, don't get angry with your parents if they don't let you and your friends drink or smoke in *your* room (which is against the law for minors anyway). Guess what? You can't do it in your dorm room either!

More importantly, if you are working, your company has employee handbooks with more rules than your student handbook. That's because employee handbooks usually include both state and federal laws, as well as your company policies. You also have to sign a form which says you understand and agree to the rules. If you break the rules, you will be **fired**. Unless you have a written contract to work at a company, you are considered an "At-will" employee. The majority of everyone working are "At-will" employees, which means that they can be fired for a good reason or *no* reason at all.

SOCIAL RESPONSIBILITY

Like I mentioned earlier, no matter what you aspire to become, you must be accountable to someone. In America, we are fortunate to live in a democracy where the government does not control *every* aspect of our being. However, the government does in fact control important areas of our lives. A few examples include: i) driving, ii) earning income, iii) voting, and iv) getting married.

i) Your Driver's License

By now you should have or be close to being eligible for a driver's license. Did you feel the stress of having the identification required just to complete the paperwork? Again, there are rules that you must follow or you will not be allowed to drive: passing a written test, practice hours behind the wheel, driving curfews, and driving probation. Driving in any state is a *privilege* and not a right. Therefore, many of you who are already on the road may have suffered the consequences of speeding, texting while driving or driving without insurance. Those are all traffic violations that result in suspension of your driving privilege. Not following state driving rules has serious consequences for future employment.

ii) Earning Income

If you are working, you have noticed that the government is taking money out of your check under the Federal Insurance Contributions Act (FICA). This is actually money set aside for your when you reach retirement age for Social Security and medical benefits. The government requires you to account for every dollar you make and expects you to file your income taxes in April of every year.

Many people have gone to jail and will continue to go to jail for not filing taxes. It is a serious federal crime. They don't just go after celebrities and athletes who make millions of dollars. Your money counts too! I know right now you think it's cool to work off the books and get cash in hand, but it will eventually catch up with your or your employer.

Being a responsible citizen means you are filing taxes on *your* earned income. It is important to learn about the tax filing process. No one really knows all the rules so don't sweat about that. A good place to get a general understanding is to start with any of the online tax interview questionnaires. Don't begin your work career evading your taxes.

iii) Voting

I cannot stress the importance of using your Constitutional right to vote. Regardless of the media opinions and other negative aspects of the political process, your right to vote is fundamental, and is one that has historically been denied to people of color. Don't get distracted by the conversations of people who say "Why vote, nothing is going to change anyway?" That's not true. Change is inevitable, whether good or bad, every political process results in change. Your vote counts! The good news is that you just need identification and proof of address to vote. There are not a lot of rules, however, you can only vote in the district you live in, even if you send in an absentee ballot. Another important point about voting is that if a person has been convicted of a felony and is incarcerated or on parole, he cannot vote. However, once he is released or is on probation, he *can* register to vote.

iv) Marriage & Other licenses

Did you know that every state has its own rules on getting a marriage license? You cannot legally get married without a license. Years ago, many states required both parties to undergo blood tests. In addition, if you want to be a doctor, lawyer, financial advisor, or several other professional occupations, there are licensing requirements with testing and additional rules that must be adhered to. If you fail to follow the licensing rules, you will lose your license to earn income in that field.

So, as you see, there is no escaping rules! Whether it be your parents' rules, school rules, work rules, or federal and state government laws and rules, your future success will be based on how you adhere to them. It doesn't matter if you are a multi-million dollar celebrity, professional athlete, president of company or the President of the United States, you must follow rules.

Download this

No adult walking this Earth can do whatever they want to do!

UNLEASHING THE KING INSIDE

As you can see, the creation of the family structure exists so that everyone has a firm foundation on understanding authority, respect, and adhering to rules. Your family provides the examples of how to interact in relationships, to help you interact with others in society. Let go of any negative emotions and disrespectful outbursts you may feel when someone in a position of authority, like your parent, teacher, or boss, requires you to do something well within your capacity. Embrace your family and fundamental rules to unleash **The King Inside**.

Next Steps: Taking King Initiatives

- Instead of bragging to family members about your manhood, take the initiative and clean your room or other areas around your house without being told. Real men don't live at home with their parents, so until you move out, be responsible and considerate of others in your household.

- Don't sit around waiting for your parents, teachers or friends to tell you about obtaining your driver's license, working papers, voting, or other life skills you will need. Take the initiative and research your state's website or other community sites for information.

- Take a minute to think about all the rules that you dislike. Whether at home, school, work, or as part of a process that you need to undergo. Write them down. Really think about what they mean, why they are important, and how you can work within those boundaries.

- Don't take for granted the privileges that come with adulthood such as obtaining a driver's license and voting.

- Regardless of what you decided to do in your career, being a good citizen and having an understanding of your social responsibility will provide you with opportunities to succeed.

App #2

Educational Foundation

"Education is the most powerful weapon which you can use to change the world."

— *Nelson Mandela*

By now, I know you are tired of hearing adults say over and over again how much you need an education. Even though you probably don't think so, it is by far the truest statement ever uttered in your presence. It is impossible to grow as an individual without an education. Most people confuse knowing how to read and write with having an education; that is literacy. It means that you are literate and can go through life reading signs, menus, directions, and writing things as necessary. However, reading and writing are the foundation to education. Without knowing these two critical skill sets, you will be at a loss when it comes to acquiring more knowledge. Education is in fact, your ability to think, reason and analyze information. Since everyone learns differently, don't be discouraged. You can learn, yet it may require the expertise of educators to supply you with the appropriate teaching method that works for you.

Education is also the key to helping you achieve your career aspirations. Whether you strive to be a teacher, doctor, architect, entrepreneur, scientist, computer programmer, or choose any other career option (there are tons to choose from), you will need an education to get started. I like to think of education as a personal investment in yourself. It's something that no one can take away from you. Another great part of acquiring an education is that the further you go, the more options you will have not only in your career, but other career fields as well. In other words, the opportunities are endless!

King's Wisdom...

"Schools fail boys in many ways...Not only are they resistant to change, many programs that are perfect for high-energy, right-brain learners, such as physical education and the arts, have been virtually eliminated in schools. Boys are excellent at doing complicated NBA math, NFL math, rap math, and drug math, yet they are failing basic math and algebra in school."

—Dr. Jawanza Kunjufu,
Educational Consultant, Author
Excerpt, Understanding
Black Male Learning Styles

Just think about it. If generations of young people decide that obtaining an education is a waste of time, how will the country grow and develop? Who will lead? Who will invent? Who will build? Who will explore? I really hope you see that having an educated society helps build a stronger country. The more knowledge you gain of the world, concepts, systems, or processes, for example, the broader your perspective will be about life and what impact you can make to an area of study.

> ## King's Wisdom...
>
> "Understand that all thinking occurs within, and across disciplines and domains of knowledge and experience. Despite having taken many classes few students are able to think biologically, chemically, geographically, historically, etc. Students study literature but do not think in a literary way. They study poetry, but do not think poetically."
>
> —Barry C. Masters
> *Project Manager, Electrical Engineer*

Having an educational foundation also helps you to mature. If you really want to get out of your "mama's house," then increase your knowledge and further your education. Once you set your plan in motion, you will begin to see your future in a positive light. You will start making key decisions about your life and career. You will ask yourself questions like, *Where do I want to live? How will I earn a living?* Education teaches you to not only ask questions, but to find answers. You don't have to take someone else's words or opinions as fact. You can study and research areas that are important to you. A clear sign of manhood is setting goals, and working hard to achieve them. One of your primary goals should be to continue your education beyond high school.

GOING PRO

My sons have been playing sports ever since they were school age. Throughout their lives, they have been involved in football and basketball. As a parent, I recognized the importance of sports in their growth and development. There is enough documented evidence to demonstrate that participating in sports is a great benefit for kids and helps promote physical, social, emotional and educational well-being up.

Yet an issue in African-American communities is that a large majority of the youth and parents are fixated on going pro. I cannot tell you the number of times I have seen parents devote their lives to their child playing a professional sport. This is a great amount of pressure on a young man; to be the savior and ultimate breadwinner of the family. Of course, becoming a professional athlete is "a beyond your wildest dreams" accomplishment, but the chances of actually making it as a professional athlete are few and far between. In fact, the chart below from the NCAA Research department compiled in 2015 shows the actual number of student-athletes going pro.

Currently, there are more than 460,000 NCAA athletes. It is important to know that only a select few in their sport actually make it to the pros or the Olympics.

Sport	NCAA Participants	Approx. Draft Eligible	# Draft Slots	#NCAA Drafted	% NCAA to Major Pro *	% NCAA to Total Pro ^
Football	71,291	15,842	256	255	1.6%	3.7%
Basketball (M)	18, 320	4,071	60	47	1.2%	11.6%
Basketball (W)	16,319	3,626	36	32	0.9%	4.7%
Baseball	33,431	7,429	1,216	638	8.6%	____
Ice Hockey (M)	3,976	884	211	60	6.8%	____
Soccer (M)	23,602	5,245	76	72	1.4%	____

Table 1.0

Source: www.ncaa.org/about/resources/research/

estimated-probability-competing-professional-athletics.

See Notes in References section.

COLLEGE BOUND

> *"... education can take you way farther*
> *than a football, baseball, track, or*
> *basketball will -that's just the bottom line."*
>
> -Bo Jackson

The good news is that according to NCAA statistics, the chances of a student-athlete earning a college degree, is much higher than student-athletes going pro. Graduation success rates for Division I schools is 84%, Division II is 72% and Division III is 87%. Those are very encouraging numbers that should help you see that playing sports is great in college, yet you have a much greater chance of graduating with a degree to help advance your future.

Although graduating from high school is a great accomplishment, it is just one step along your educational journey. Going to college should be part of your game plan. Without a college degree, you will not be able to compete for the next level jobs and careers. Many high school graduates have a false sense of security when they get their first jobs. They think that having money in their pocket now is what life's all about. It's only natural for your current paycheck to seem like it can go a long way if you are living at home-without the responsibilities of paying necessary bills. The money you earn with a high school diploma when compared to your earning potential with a college degree, may be several times more. Research these statistics on your own, and you will see that college is absolutely worth it in the long run.

King's Wisdom...

"Our educational system is in a "state of emergency" as many individuals will never be in a position to navigate successfully. Not because they lack the "intelligence" needed to matriculate, but simply lack of exposure. Who's to blame? There are some conversations that are difficult to have as a result of the content/context. However, in order to grow, such narratives have to emerge. Don't hide behind the "I can't" mindset because it will only reinforce your here and now circumstances. It's never too late to learn something new."

—Don Trahan, Jr., Ph.D., NCC
Diversity and Inclusion Specialist

Today, our economy is not heavily based on manufacturing as it was several years ago. Many large manufacturing companies outsource their productions overseas. Technology has taken over every aspect of our lives. As you see, our economy will be more knowledge-based. That means, you will earn more based on what you know and how beneficial it is to society.

> **OUTSOURCING:** When one company hires another company, usually overseas, to handle all of the manufacturing and distribution of their product or service.

My final plug on the importance of going to college is that you will be exposed to people from different cultures, races and ethnicities. Assimilating with a global community of students will help you learn to interact and work with others. We live in a global environment. You need to recognize that the further you go in your career and education, that everyone is not going to look like you. Therefore, open your mind to the social aspect of assimilating with your future colleagues. Many of your college relationships can turn into lifetime connections that can help you throughout your career.

i) College Costs

Unfortunately, going to college is very expensive. But don't let that discourage you from applying to as many scholarships, grants and other financial aid available. Your college search is not something that you should look into your senior year. You should develop a plan by your sophomore year of the schools you want to attend. The more you know about their costs, SAT/ACT requirements, and any other information you need to make a decision, the better prepared you will be to implement your plan. At the end of this book there are college resources for you to research for more information.

ii) College Major

Some schools offer thousands of subjects to major in. The key is to lean towards a major that involves doing something that you like or are actually really good at. There are tons of careers that require skills that you already have. Research careers in order to find a few that interest you. Choosing a major is not a once in a lifetime decision. It's OK to change your major down the line. You will never know if a career is for you until you explore it on the college level, and even in the marketplace. Additional college resources and readiness information are provided at the end of this book.

Download this

There is no shortcut or substitute for furthering your education after high school. Focus on your grades, put in the required time and effort, and you will have more career options at your disposal.

VOCATIONAL EDUCATION

Trust me, I get it, college is not for everyone. I've heard so many of my students echo these words and I totally agree. Everyone learns differently. However, you still need to have an employable skill, a plan, and a good work ethic. It's tough out there. Not to mention the negative stereotypes widely circulated in society about your future.

Over the years, the statistics remain the same; black male college graduation rates are low when compared to white males. The positive news is that more black males are enrolled in college, yet for various reasons, they do not finish. So, if you decide that college is not for you, then fine, but you *should* attend a trade school to learn a skill that will provide you with earned income. You cannot have a productive life without earned money in your pocket.

The job market is still competitive and college graduates struggle to find jobs. Many end up underemployed or taking a job outside of their major. The good news is that there are a number of alternatives to earning a college degree, especially online courses and other certifications. Find out what interests you and what you really enjoy doing. There are trade schools across the country that provide hands-on training for those interested in automotive, computers, construction, electrical, and other careers.

For those of you who choose not to attend college, there is an opportunity to educate yourself in an area that interests you because of the wealth of information online. Your knowledge in a particular field could land you a job. The key is for you to commit to learning something new.

UNLEASHING THE KING INSIDE

Learning is a never-ending process. Whether it is learning in school, learning more in your career, or learning about life, it is continuous. Everyone has special gifts and talents. It is up to you to discover what yours are. The more you research and explore career options, the better prepared you will be when it is time to choose your college. Knowledge is power. Strive to increase your knowledge to unleash **The King Inside**.

Next Steps: Taking King Initiatives

- Research internships, college scholarships, and career-related websites to assist you in finding opportunities to advance your interests.

- Set realistic goals in order to accomplish them to continue your momentum.

- Don't allow distractions to get in the way of your schoolwork. Confide in someone you trust to help you handle it.

- The bottom line is this: the longer you stay in school the more options you have in life. The shorter you stay in school, the fewer options you have in life.

- Consider Co-Op programs which allow you to attend college and work in a career you are interested in.

- Education is something that no one can take away from you. Wear your accomplishments with pride.

App #3

Spiritual Foundation

*"The key to success is to keep growing
in all areas of life — mental, emotional,
spiritual as well as physical."*

— Julius "Dr. J" Erving

As young men, you probably have not given much thought about your spirituality unless you regularly attend a church, temple, mosque or other place of worship. Spirituality in a general sense is realizing that we are connected to something much bigger than ourselves. It is an experience that everyone can relate to as we tap into that inner voice to provide comfort, peace and direction. Many find it through prayer. Others find it through meditation, in nature, or a physical activity. The main takeaway is that when you connect with your spirituality, you should have a better understanding of who you are.

Keep in mind that religion and spirituality are not the same thing. Even though spirituality may have some elements of religion tied to it, they are not the same. Religion often times is based on a written doctrine that helps you to determine right and wrong, for example. Spirituality, on the other hand, helps you personally find the meaning of life. It is also connected to your emotional health and well-being, and is based on the premise of being in a positive state of mind to allow you to see things clearer or from another perspective.

You can find a sense of spirituality listening to relaxing music or reading inspirational books. Basically, anything that touches you on the inside and makes you feel a sense of peace during or right after the moment can be considered spiritual. Your interactions and connections with others can also be spiritual.

I certainly cannot speak for everyone, but my spirituality gives me a sense of purpose and direction for my life. It is important for you to find your spiritual foundation as well. I believe my personal growth and connection to others is a result of my spirituality. It keeps me grounded and reminds me that "it's not all about me" and that I am here to somehow help others, which is something that makes me feel fulfilled. That is why I chose a career in teaching. The idea of giving back and helping young people achieve their dreams is my driving force.

I think spirituality is difficult to put in words because it is a feeling. However, like anything worth doing, it takes some type of intentional action to get better at it and to be focused. The more you pay attention to your environment and just take in the sights, sounds, and smells around you, the more mindful you will become of your environment. Each day dedicate a few minutes of quiet time to take in your surroundings and enjoy the moment.

King's Wisdom...

If you are described as a person that has spiritual well-being, it means that you are able to
mesh your purpose in life through your connection with self, others, the arts, and nature.
You truly understand that there is a power
greater than yourself.

What's Your Moral Compass?

The term "moral compass" refers to your decision-making in determining right from wrong. It is
your inner voice that guides you. Hopefully, you have
developed a moral compass to do the right thing.
By now, you should have a clear sense as to what is
right and what is wrong.

As you will see, life is all about the personal decisions you make. The more good decisions you act
upon, the better your chances of success. On the
flip side, the more bad decisions you engage in, the
fewer opportunities you will have for your future. So
when your crew picks you up in a stolen car and you
know they have drugs or weapons in the car, your
decision to engage in a joy ride is flat out bad. It can
cost you lengthy jail time.

Engaging in any type of illegal activity is ultimately the wrong decision. No matter how great the money is, you will eventually get caught. The more times you get away with something, the harder it will be for you to stop. It becomes a bad habit that feels too good to break. The key is to not get involved. Why don't you be the one to put holes in the negative stereotypes that you are destined to become a criminal? How many current and former convicts does each generation need to realize that selling drugs or guns, committing murder, or participating in other criminal activity is literally throwing your life away? It's selling yourself short before you really get a chance to experience the good things life has to offer.

Having a good moral compass is the only way to survive. The temptation to do wrong is so easy and it is everywhere. Corruption is rampant in politics, business, school systems, and even religious institutions. Money and greed will continue to be the fall of people. You are stronger than you think. Resist the temptation to do wrong.

MEDITATION

The more time you spend observing and relaxing in your environment, the easier it will be for you to begin the practice of meditation. I have read that there is actually scientific evidence to show how your brain changes the longer you meditate. There is a great deal of information to verify that being still every day for at least 15-30 minutes can make a big difference in how things affect you and your interaction with others.

Meditation helps you to become calm about things that the average person who does not meditate may find offensive or angered. Practicing it daily will literally shift your focus from yourself and give you a desire to connect and help others. I think researching how meditation can change your brain for the better is definitely something worth looking into. Spirituality and meditation deal with your mind.

In order to be effective in your daily life and personal growth, you must not only work on improving your mind, but also your body.

YOU ARE WHAT YOU EAT

Just like you are never too young to tap into your spiritual side, you are also never too young to pay attention to what you feed your body. I've seen boys in my school first thing in the morning drinking orange soda and eating Swedish Fish. What a shock to your system! There are so many studies which show that breakfast is the most important meal that you can eat before school. Unfortunately, most kids skip a nutritious breakfast and settle for junk food or nothing. What most kids don't realize is that eating properly helps you to develop mentally and physically. When your body does not get the proper nutrients, you won't feel good and your moods will be off balance.

To be at your best health, every day, make sure you get the right amount protein (eggs, fish, chicken, vegetables), carbohydrates (fruits, vegetables, potatoes, pasta, rice), and fruit. Protein helps your muscles, hair, skin, eyes and internal organs. Basically, you need protein to grow. Our bodies also need the right amount of fat to be healthy. There are both good and bad fats. Good fats include nuts, fresh tuna and salmon. Bad fats are found in those produced from animals like dairy products and meats which should be eaten in moderation.

Try eating healthy/balanced meals and see if it makes a difference in your energy level as well as sharpen your mind. Try your best to cut out the sugary drinks and soda as continued use can increase your risk of type 2 diabetes, high blood pressure, obesity or other health ailments that disproportionately affect African-Americans.

EXERCISE

Many of you have already played sports since you

were in elementary school. How are you going to keep active when you graduate high school? Did you know that health experts recommend that young men your age get at least one hour of physical activity each day? Unfortunately, for most teenagers, once they drop out of organized sports they lack the drive to workout, or get involved in physical activities. As I have mentioned earlier, everyone is not going to make it to the pros or even playing on an international level. Therefore, eating right and getting the proper exercise will put you in a great position to handle the hard work and commitment needed to move to the next level.

If you played basketball, join a local YMCA to both work out and play pickup games a few days a week. For football, soccer, and baseball players, research the adult leagues in your area and join a team. If you are in college, nearly every sport has an intramural league as well. At the end of the day, your life is in your hands. It is really up to you to research, ask questions, and take the initiative in improving your overall health.

UNLEASHING THE KING INSIDE

The topics touched upon in this section may appear to be over the head of young men your age. Yet, I think it is important to for you to know that there is a spiritual side to all of us that should guide us toward personal growth. More important, your overall physical health will be a key factor in your pursuit of success at any level. Learn more about your mind, body, and spirit to unleash **The King Inside**.

Download this

Don't wait until you are "old" to improve your mind, body, and spirit. The sooner you tune into your mind and body by feeding it positivity and the proper nutrients, your attitude and emotions will lead to a more productive day.

Next Steps: Taking King Initiatives

- Check out the local YMCA in your area for information on membership. There are discounts for students, and you will have the opportunity to work with nutritionists, and other trainers to set you on a healthy path.

- Try to spend at least 20 minutes a day of quiet time to reduce stress and clear your mind.

- Cut back on junk food and try to eat three balanced meals a day. Skipping breakfast or lunch deprives your body and brain of the nourishment you need to focus in school.

- Join a like-minded group to give you the support needed to keep up your healthy activities.

• Take notes about your overall energy, concentration, and grades to see how you have improved with your new healthy mind and body routine.

App #4

Mentorship Foundation

"Surround yourself with people who take their work seriously, but not themselves, those who work hard and play hard."

— *Colin Powell*

As a single mother of two young men, I recognize the importance of having a father as a positive role model in their lives. There is enough research to demonstrate that boys cannot learn to be men from their mothers. Of course, mom plays a key role in shaping their son's lives, but we cannot provide the balance that both genders can offer to help you grow to your fullest potential. For boys who are fortunate to have a father in the home, statistics also show that there is an average of 10-minute one-on-one interaction with their sons.[1]

This is not nearly enough time to bond and impart necessary life skills. The bottom line is that young men without fathers in the home need more male mentor role models than ever before.

What exactly is a mentor? Did you know that the word "mentor" came from the ancient Greek poem, written by Homer, called *The Odyssey*? Many of you may have read this in your English class. In the poem, Odysseus, the King of Ithaca, had to fight in the Trojan War and asked his trusted friend, Mentor, to watch over his son Telemachus. Odysseus was gone for 20 years and finally made it back home to his family. Throughout his absence, Mentor served as a teacher

---

1. firstthings.org/importance-of-positive-male-role-models/

and overseer of Odysseus' son and household.

> **MENTOR:** A person with experience in a particular field who guides a less experienced person to aid them in fulfilling their goals. Mentors should be positive role models and actively engaged in helping the mentee.
>
> **MENTEE:** A person who receives advice and direction from a mentor.

Having a mentor as a young man as well as when you are an adult, can be beneficial to your personal growth. Mentors can expose you to careers, provide inside knowledge and access to opportunities that you may never receive or be aware of. Keep in mind that a mentor-mentee relationship is a two-way street. The mentor must be willing to commit to interacting with the mentee and provide good advice in a variety of life-skill areas as well as exposure to the marketplace. By the same token, the mentee, must be willing to receive advice and instruction and follow through on scheduled calls, meetings, or assignments.

All too often African-American males are inundated with false images of male role models of athletes, rappers, and other celebrities who have "made it" out of the hood. Many want to imitate that perceived level of success. Instead, these young men need to be connected to teachers, engineers, businessmen, doctors, lawyers, architects, and other successful men who have endured hardships, disappointments, and other setbacks, yet continued to work hard to attain their careers. Young men like yourselves, need to see first-hand that you have to pay your dues. The idea of instant success and your name in lights is unrealistic. As a mentee, you need to hang out and be fully engaged with men who have attained their goals both personally and professionally. Seeing these real-life examples of the necessary steps for success can change the statistical negative trajectory of your life.

By now, you're probably asking yourself, *How do I find a mentor*? That's a good question and the answer is that they are probably right under your nose. A mentor can be your neighbor, a teacher, or any adult that is working in an area that you may desire as a future career. In addition, keep in mind that you may seek mentors for different areas of your life. For example, you may want an academic mentor who can help you with school work, study tips, college planning, and anything related to your educational growth. A business mentor, on the other hand, can provide insight into the business world. This person may also serve as your personal mentor who will be engaged in your personal growth and development as a productive citizen.

King's Wisdom...

"Although I did not have a mentor growing up, I did however, have a village of men around me that set great examples and provided me with positive outlets which kept me on the straight and narrow path. For example, there was Mr. Lewis who organized youth basketball leagues in my community. He showed me what it meant to have passion for young people and provide them with a fun, positive outlet. I believe I was channeling my inner Mr. Lewis when I developed an after school basketball mentoring and self-development program for at risk boys. It was also men like Pastor Earl, my spiritual grandfather. His influence and my respect for him kept me out of trouble. These men and others were great extensions to my mother, who was the chief architect in making me the man I am today. I don't have a professional mentor, but I am always looking for one."

—George Stewart II,
Educator, Youth Program Developer

Choosing a Mentor

In order for your relationship with your mentor to work it is important that you consider the following:

- Know which type of mentor you are looking for;

- Make a list of the things you want to learn from the mentor or questions you have about their career path;

- Request reasonable times to meet or schedule calls;

- Be prompt for all meetings and calls;

- Complete any required assignments;

- Update your mentor on your progress; and

- Thank your mentor often for their time.

Download this

A good mentor-mentee relationship provides the mentee with a long-term plan for the future. The mentor should work with you to set goals and help you reach them.

King's Wisdom...

"Develop a sense of SELF, seek mentors in the field you aspire to go into, join community mentoring organizations, develop a sense of financial independence, and most of all RESPECT others. "

—Dr. Ricky A. Gallaway
President/CEO
Transcontinental Consulting

Mentoring Matters

It's no surprise that some of the most successful people in history, business, sports, or entertainment had mentors. In fact, former Morehouse College President, Dr. Benjamin Mays was a mentor to Dr. Martin Luther King, Jr. when King was an undergraduate at Morehouse. As a leader of the Civil Rights Movement, Dr. King, in turn, mentored Jesse Jackson, Congressman John Lewis, and countless others. Dr. King also sought mentorship from Mahatma Gandhi, the leader of India's non-violent independence movement.

Several professional athletes credit their college and high school coaches as their mentors, including Michael Jordan, Dwayne Wade, and Kobe Bryant. All three athletes currently mentor other NBA rookies. From a musical standpoint, the legendary Ray Charles was a mentor to Quincy Jones. Jones has mentored a large number of artists in various music genres and has given the world some of the most successful music of all time, in his work with artists like Michael Jackson. Last, but certainly not least, several extraordinary people from all walks of life and professions credit their parents or a family member's mentorship as the key to their success.

Download this

Without a committed mentor, many of our great leaders, athletes, and artists may never have achieved greatness and changed the course of history as we know it.

UNLEASHING THE KING INSIDE

There is no question that mentorship is a necessary element to helping good people become great. The more positive people that pour into your life, the higher your chances are for success in attaining lifelong dreams. Seriously consider reaching out to a mentor regardless of your age or educational level. There is nothing more valuable than walking with someone who has been there before. Someone who can guide and help you attain your goals. Begin working on your mentors list to unleash **The King Inside**.

Next Steps: Taking King Initiatives

- Think of mentoring as your first real step at networking in your future career. The more connections and contacts you build now, the better your chances of landing opportunities in today's extremely competitive workplace.

- It's OK to have more than one mentor. Seek out mentors for your specific desires: academic, career, life experiences, or a combination of skill sets.

- Choose someone you admire and respect.

- Don't be discouraged if you cannot find a mentor right away. It may take time. However, use your time wisely to focus on your studies and research careers.

- Talk about your future plans with your teachers, school counselors, and other experienced individuals who are in a position to offer advice on steps to take to reach your goals.

App #5

Friends Foundation

*"You can't build anything with a flimsy foundation.
Friendship is the foundation."*

— *Hill Harper*

The word "friend" is such a common term that I believe many use often or too loosely to describe a person they have only known for a short while. A friend is someone that you have built an established relationship of trust. He or she is someone who supports you, and has your best interest at heart. Friendships are very important at every age and level you achieve in life. As young men, your friends probably rank higher than your family. Although typical at this stage in life, it is important to recognize the need and role that each group plays in your future success.

Most teens seem to think that they have no choice in choosing their friends. So many times I have intervened in situations with young men who were in some type of trouble both inside and outside of school, and when I speak to one of them individually, I asked "What are you doing hanging out with him anyway? You know he's not the type of person to make good decisions." The response is usually, "I don't know. He always does some crazy stuff. I don't know why I am his friend." "Well now you are in trouble for being with your friend while he was doing crazy stuff." It's really up to you to take the initiative and choose your friends. Friendship should be reciprocal: both parties are giving and receiving from the relationship. There are certain characteristics in a person that may appeal to you, and those positive qualities are what you should look for.

First, friends should have something in common to connect and build upon in your interactions. Why would you want to hang around someone who does not like or engage in anything that is important to you? How much fun can you get out of following someone else's desires and goals? I know it can be difficult figuring out what you like to do, however, I bet there are things that your "friends" are doing right now that you know you *don't* like or want to do.

Second, choose a friend who is honest with you and others. Again, friendships are built on trust, so someone who is trustworthy and is respected by their peers, teachers, and other adults is a great friend to have. On the flip side, the disrespectful, trouble-maker, is not someone you want to be associated with. Even if you are not like your friend, you will be guilty of having his or her same negative characteristics, and written off as a challenge to deal with.

Third, a good friend is someone who understands you more than others. Everyone has their own weird habits and quirks. Your friend should be able to laugh with you and not at you. Stick with someone who has a similar sense of humor and is comfortable around you and in groups. A friend is someone who is happy to see you succeed and is willing to help you any way he can. If that means helping you study for a test or ensuring that you are on time for work, that person is a great friend.

Finally, a true friend is someone who is there for you during the good and bad times. So often our friendships are put to the test when one person's situation changes either financially, physically, or relationally. You have probably witnessed the guy at school with the car who has all the friends, both guys and girls. When his car is in the shop and he can't afford to get it out, he is not as popular. If he plays a sport and gets hurt, no one stops by after the game to check on him or to just hang out until he gets back on his feet. It's so easy to be a friend when everything is going exactly how you want it. It takes great character to be a friend when you are really needed. Choose a friend who will stick with you when things don't turn out as either of you planned.

Download this

Take the lead in choosing your friends. If you both have common interests, the connection will be genuine. Forcing yourself on someone or someone forcing himself into your circle, will create unnecessary tension and stress. Fake friendships will ultimately distract you from achieving your goals.

King's Wisdom...

"A healthy relationship is one where all parties involved benefit and are made better as a result of being together. That doesn't mean there will not be conflict or disagreement, but all parties know that they are safe to be transparent and vulnerable."

—Darnell Weathersby
Motivational Speaker, Published Author
LeadOne LLC/ School Administrator

Unfortunately, many of you may be surrounded by a negative environment in your schools and neighborhoods. As tough as it may be, there are many success stories of young men in your situation who have gone on to reach their dreams and make an impact on their communities. Take a look at the three friends from Newark, New Jersey. They are known as The Three Doctors: Drs. Sampson Davis, Rameck Hunt and George Jenkins. Each one overcame a hardship that you may be going through. These three friends made a pact that they would all go to college and become doctors. They were accountable to each other and encouraged each other along the way. Today they are certified doctors in New Jersey specializing in a medical field. The Three Doctors are also authors. You should pick up one of their books to learn how they managed to succeed against the odds. They are a tough act to follow, but make your own pact with your friends to be better.

Friend Clashes

Have you experienced tension in your home when your family members don't like your friends? How did you handle it? As a parent, I have had concerns with some of my sons friends over the years. It's a difficult position to be in because I knew if I constantly warned my sons or even forbade them from hanging out with someone that I disliked was likely to drive them to hang more with the "bad influence" person.

Over time, I learned how to engage those friends I had concerns with to gain credibility with my sons that eventually demonstrated their need to cut them off on their own. I also realized that the more I encouraged my sons and provided positive feedback, that their self-esteem grew and I noticed their choice of friends were in line with their personalities and upbringing.

UNLEASHING THE KING INSIDE

All relationships require some form of compromise. You must be willing to bend in areas that are not as important to you, but are very important to your friend. Choose your friends wisely. Look for those who share your same interests as well as having your best interest at heart. It is important to have someone besides your family to talk to and help you make good decisions on a regular basis. Strive to be that true friend who shows himself friendly, to unleash **The King Inside**.

Next Steps: Taking King Initiatives

- Consider your current friends. Determine whether their friendship is a help or hindrance to you. If you decide that some of your friendships are worth severing, do so in a positive manner. Use your previous hangout time to better yourself in a certain area.

- Regardless of your character, people will judge you by the friends you hang out with. Other's perception of you will be their reality and it will be difficult to change their minds about you. Stay true to yourself.

- Trying to imitate someone else is a lot of work.

- Learn to forgive your friends. True friendship will go through rocky times.

- Treat your friends *better* than how you want to be treated.

App #6

Self-Empowerment Foundation

*"One important key to success is self-confidence.
An important key to self-confidence is preparation."*

— *Arthur Ashe*

We talked about the importance of having some type of spiritual compass to guide us through life, as well as to provide insight into who we really are on the inside. Knowing who you are, and valuing yourself is a major part of walking into your manhood. The more knowledgeable you become about your cultural history, your likes and dislikes, the better equipped you will be to make purposeful decisions about your future. Self-empowerment is image-forming. It will cause you to operate with a boldness and determination to succeed at reaching your goals.

> **SELF-EMPOWERMENT:** Looking within yourself with a confident awareness of your abilities to help you set realistic goals to fulfill your destiny. Knowing the strength of your self-worth will help you make informed decisions and access opportunities. Empowerment means becoming powerful. You have the power to control your life. It's really in your own hands!

When you gain a serious understanding that you can control, to a large extent, the things that happen in your life, your self-confidence will grow. Of course, there will be things that affect us which we have no control over, but learning how to handle them will be the key to your power. Empowerment brings you a sense of peace.

To maintain balance and peace in your walk, it is helpful to rely on positive affirmations. Whether they are affirmations from others or ones you have created yourself, repeat them often throughout the day, especially as you face conflict or turmoil. Here are a few affirmations to get you going:

1. I am great. Greatness is in me and success is within my reach.

2. The word "can't" doesn't exist in my daily vocabulary.

3. I am responsible for the outcome of my life.

4. I will not make excuses for not giving my best.

5. I will control my anger in uncomfortable or challenging situations.

Take the limits off your dreams in life. Speak positive affirmations to give you the confidence and power to open and walk through any door you imagined.

CHARACTER

> *"Life is a menu so remember whoever
> and whatever you order for your life is
> what's gonna be delivered to your table."*
>
> — *Tyrese*

We all have something unique within that make others want to interact with us. That special something is called character. Your character is based on your thought process and moral values. How you handle daily situations are the signs of shaping or building your character. All of your character traits cultivate your personality. When you complete applications for jobs or school, all of your activities and interests give the decision-maker a peek into your character.

Even though we are born with certain character traits, focus on the good ones and make them part of your daily habits. Regardless of your background, once you realize what your good habits are, continue to improve upon them. The more self-awareness you recognize the better you can become. Rid yourself of those bad habits that you know are holding you back from your destiny. If you are known as a responsible, hard working person, then your likelihood of success at whatever you put your mind or hand to, is greater than someone who is irresponsible and lazy.

Whether you realize it or not, someone is always watching you, either up close or from a distance. Over time, these same people will make a judgement about you based on your actions or inaction. Do you use profanity often? Do you get angry easily? Are you honest? The more positive characteristics you have, the more likely people will gravitate towards you for friendship or other opportunities. Likewise, the more negative characteristics you display, the more likely you will be written off and labeled as someone to stay away from.

King's Wisdom...

"A young man must learn that every test, obstacle, situation, battle, adversary or fight can be conquered strategically. Sometimes bowing out of a fight may be the best strategy. Too many young men have lost their lives because they were taught to fight a battle without the proper artillery, skill, equipment or capacity to win."

—Roger A Mitchell Jr. MD
Excerpt from "The Price of Freedom: A Son's Journey"

Take a moment to consider the following positive character traits. How do you stack up? Do many of them describe you?

- Honest
- Loyal
- Kind

- Ambitious

- Patient

- Determined

- Persistent

- Cooperative

- Optimistic

- Humorous

Now take a moment to check out a few negative character traits. Do any of these describe you? If so, what steps will you take to improve or grow?

- Dishonest

- Rude

- Disrespectful

- Impatient

- Angry

- Selfish

Unfortunately, anger and bullying are a major concern for young males. You may have anger management issues if you find yourself quickly getting angry over minor things, physically hitting someone, constantly shouting, cursing, and acting recklessly. If you believe you have an anger problem, talk with a teacher, parent or other adult to seek help. Don't be discouraged if you have more negative than positive character traits at this stage in your life. There is always time to work on the negative. Recognizing how they are hindering you from success is a powerful first step for change.

King's Wisdom...

"I am far more patient now then I was when I was younger. This lesson has helped me to withstand the ups and downs of life. I recognize now that everything has its season and that I have to understand that and allow life to develop instead of trying to force things to happen under my own terms and timeline.

—Hon. Troy Singleton
Assembly 7th District, NJ

Reputation vs. Character

If you think about it another way, your character can be thought of as what's going on inside you that make up your personality. From the outside, your actions and what others say about you will create your reputation. Having a good reputation will give you advantages and leverage in life.

Even though, most people would say that it doesn't matter what others think about them, there are valid arguments on both sides.

For one thing, you need to consider your relationship with the person. Is it a family member? Is it a trusted friend? Is it someone whom you believe dislikes you? Is it a reputable person in the community? Is it a person who is a decision-maker in your employment? Again, all of these factors should weigh into your decision as to whether that person's opinion of you is fair or carries malicious intent. On the other hand, don't go overboard trying to please everyone, because no matter how hard you try, everyone is just not going to like you for some reason.

Just like character, if you don't have a great reputation, you can start by building it with people like your teachers, employer, and even your family and friends.

Appearance

I am not here to tell you which career you should choose, but I definitely want to convey that getting an education will open more doors to your future. Therefore, whether you want to work in corporate America or work with your hands in construction, your choice of clothing will matter at some point. Regardless of your career path, owning at least one dark suit for an interview or other event should be a part of your wardrobe.

With so many fashion trends today, it is difficult to keep up with the latest fashions. Not to mention the high price people are willing to pay for designer clothes and sneakers. Unfortunately, you will be judged by your clothing and personal hygiene. Your appearance is really a big deal in how people treat you. So take pride in how you look and smell, because your reputation will take on a life of its own, either positive or negative.

As a mother of two sons and an educator, I can honestly say I have an issue with young men in saggin' pants. This is probably the one fashion trend that I would love to see our culture immediately put an end to. At times, I feel as though I am being stubborn with my no saggin' tolerance stance in my home, but it is extremely difficult for me to understand how showing your backside all day is a positive thing. Call me old-fashioned. Today, there are local municipalities that have ordinances against people wearing saggin' pants. If you violate the ordinance, you will have to pay a fine. I'm not sure how effective this will be, but it is an example of how fed up people are with this fashion trend.

If you look at the big picture, your image is too important for you to not care about. Hiring managers, school admissions counselors, and others in a position to help further your career goals, will have a negative perception of you if you are not dressed appropriately (pants pulled up to your waist and casual shirt) for the occasion or opportunity. Get into the habit of looking your best each day.

WORKING

"It's all about the work...
Nothing is going to fall in your lap."
— Russell Simmons

Getting a job at this age in your life is a great way to prepare for your work career. The saying, "Hard work never killed anyone," is applicable to any career path. Success requires hard work on the field, on stage, in an office, or other employable environments. There really are no shortcuts. Developing a work ethic at a young age can be beneficial. While you are in high school, whether you start earning money mowing lawns, shoveling snow, doing odd jobs and then getting into retail, your work mindset and attitude begin to take shape.

Many psychologists and sociologists argue that working as a teen takes focus away from your studies. As a proponent of education, I encourage doing your best in school to get to the next level. However, there is a great benefit to acquiring life skills early on. Learning how to apply for a job, work, earn money, communicate, and help solve problems with those outside your circle, are invaluable. Working gives you a sense of independence and broadens your financial decision-making in buying the things you need.

Another plus for working is that it teaches responsibility and can help you with time management. Keep in mind that I am not saying that you need to work a ton of hours to have money to buy the latest designer gear, so that you come to school tired and sleep all day. Your grades will definitely suffer, which will make finishing school harder, or likely take longer.

Skills

Since you are just entering the workforce, the skills needed are general, likable, social skills. No matter what field you enter, having excellent communication skills will help further your career. Your ability to work well in teams and help resolve conflict, are other key skill sets that the majority of employers seek. It also helps to be a good listener and know how to follow instructions. Are you good with managing your time? Time management is a skill that the most skilled professionals often lack. You are in a great position to hone your time management skills as you juggle between school, extracurricular activities, volunteering, and work. Employers want to see that you are doing what is expected of you during your time spent on their premises.

SOCIAL MEDIA

The popularity and lifeline of social media cannot be overstated. Billions of people are online every day, exposing personal details of their life for the world to view. Whether you are on Facebook, Twitter, Instagram, Vine, Periscope, or other social sites, the global community will continue broadcasting "news" into the social media frenzy. Think twice before you hit "Send."

We have become obsessed with "self" and are fixated on photographing or videotaping our entire day. Unfortunately, some parts of our day are not a good reflection of our character. Posting photos, videos, comments or other content that may be viewed as offensive, can hinder your job prospects, college opportunities, and future. Even if you delete your posts, chances are your followers sent it out to others.

Today, employers are viewing online social media accounts of candidates for employment. Your social media account will tell a hiring manager a lot about your personality, outlook in life, and shows whether you know how to act professionally. Americans are competing for jobs and higher education on a global scale, which makes it harder to land your dream job or dream school. If an employer or admissions counselor visits your social media page and you are posting messages with a lot of profanity, pictures and videos of yourself or others drunk or engaged in confrontations, your chances of being chosen are low. Since you are ultimately accountable for your character and reputation, I urge you again to think twice before you post something on social media that may negatively affect your future.

Pros

There are so many benefits to using social media in a positive way. Having a social network support group of actual friends and then hundreds or thousands of like-minded "friends" is a great self-esteem builder. The opportunity to instantly communicate and connect with others globally on issues that affect your generation is invaluable. Learning how to create content, organize people, articulate ideas, and strategize, are skills that will help further your career.

As a young male, your social media activism has changed outcomes of various current events in recent history. From President Obama's two-term election, Trayvon Martin, Eric Garner, Mike Brown, Freddie Gray, Sandra Bland, and many others. Your voice in open discussions, organized marches and other awareness campaigns, have been outstanding. The world is on notice that there is more to you than the negative media portrayals. More change is needed.

Another benefit of using social media is that it gives you the opportunity to learn about things that you may not know have existed. It can take you out of your comfort zone and open yourself up to more possibilities. Equally important, is knowing how to navigate online, adapting to new technology and effectively interacting with others is a key skill set that employers seek.

UNLEASHING THE KING INSIDE

I cannot emphasize it enough—your future is in your hands. There is a leader, a thinker, a change agent, destined to come forth. You have the power to achieve your goals. Self-empowerment comes from within. Having the confidence to dream big and take the steps to achieve those dreams is a good initiative. It comes from showcasing your good habits and working to rid yourself from the bad ones. It means that you care about your reputation and will do things necessary to ensure it remains positive. It means dressing for the occasion and being mindful of your language. It means creating and saying positive affirmations to motivate you throughout the day. It means, holding your head high because you know who you are, as you unleash **The King Inside**.

Next Steps: Taking King Initiatives

- If you had a reputation of being late and not being prepared for school or work, focus on changing that reality and perception by being on-time, well-prepared and handing in your school assignments early. Do a little more than is expected of you at work.

- Be a person of your word. So many people say one thing and do another, or commit to something and not see it through. Be dedicated to your goals.

- To build your character and reputation, go out of your way to help others. Demonstrate your lack of selfishness, which is a challenge for most people.

- Take pride in your appearance and hygiene. Your parents already taught you this. Listen.

- Hold your head high and walk with a purpose. Your body language says a lot about you. Always remember that someone is watching you.

- Don't use language or post things on your social media accounts that your parents would not be proud of.

App #7

Money Foundation

"Focusing your life solely on making a buck shows a certain poverty of ambition. It asks too little of yourself. Because it's only when you hitch your wagon to something larger than yourself that you realize your true potential."

—*President Barack Obama*

By now you are concerned about money. Understanding the value of money and how to manage it is a learned process. We just don't automatically know what to do with it. Our instinct is to spend it as soon as it touches our hands or shows up in our bank account. Most teenagers are caught up in the "want" phase and want every new gadget, clothing, sneakers, or other new thing that comes along. Working within a budget is not something that feels good, yet it is probably one of the most important skills you can acquire and master.

Financial knowledge is not something taught in the majority of schools today, so it is up to you to learn about it on your own. I say this because, realistically your parents may not have been taught. Nearly all financial experts advise you to pay yourself first. Whether you get an allowance, gift money or a paycheck, always put aside something for yourself for the future.

As you get older, your expenses are greater. If we took our focus off the clothing and other fads, teen expenses like organized sports or other activities outside of school, as well as special school events like banquets, proms, and trips add up quickly. This is also a time when you start dating and going out with your friends on weekends. Paying for your date and pitching in for gas or your own car expenses can be tough. There are a few money lessons where experts agree:

i) Earning Income: If you work after school and on weekends, decide how you are going to save and spend your paycheck *before* you get it. Open both a savings and checking account. You should also get a debit card to help curb your spending habits; you can't spend what you don't have. However, don't link your debit card to your savings or you will find yourself broke by transferring funds on your phone between both accounts. Many banks require a guardian to sign off on withdrawals if you are under age 18.

ii) Create a Budget: Write out your spending needs for the week or every two weeks depending on your pay period. Subtract your expenses from your income. With state and federal taxes, you will see that you don't have as much as you thought. Chances are you will have a shortfall. What things can you do or cut out to break even, or put aside for savings?

iii) Saving for the future: Make a list of things you desire for the future. Pay yourself and stick to your budget to purchase the item. Don't deplete your savings all at once. Be patient.

a) Saving for retirement, IRAs, 401Ks, etc.

With the high cost of living today, it is difficult for most people to save, let along think about saving for their future. Even though you are young, familiarizing yourself with retirement concepts will expose you to a few common saving options. Many employers offer 401(k) retirement savings plans which require you to contribute a specific amount from your paycheck each pay period. This is a good "forced" way to save without taxes being taken out, until you withdraw the money.

Some employers match your contributions as well. If you choose to work in an educational field, a non-profit organization, or hospital cooperative, your employer will likely offer a 403(b) retirement savings plan with similar functions as a 401(k). Keep in mind that the terms 401(k) and 403(b) all refer to that particular section of the Internal Revenue Code. Each of these sections provides a lot of detail on the maximum contributions and other rules for opening an account to receive tax benefits under that code.

There are other employer plans, as well as special plans for business owners, so make sure you inquire about additional options to see which plan will work best for you. As an individual, other retirement saving options such as an IRA or a Roth IRA can be purchased from your bank or other financial institution. Saving for retirement and investing can be both confusing and rewarding. Make sure you review the plan information and then talk with your employer's human resources department or a local financial professional, before you open any type of retirement savings account, as there are risks involved.

Download this

Make learning how to manage your money a priority. Read books on money management and use the available tools and apps to help get you started on the right track.

Independent Living

As a teenager, I could not wait to get out of my parents' house. I thought having my own place would be the best thing in the world. I was wrong. Living on your own is a huge responsibility. First, you have to be great at budgeting and sticking to it. The due date for bills come around quickly; rent, car insurance, electricity, cable, cell phone, groceries, gas, or other necessities. What about those who have student loans and credit card debt? Do you realize that on any given month, six or more bills could be due around the same time? How can you afford to pay them?

I recall being short on funds every month. I asked my dad for money often. I did not have a plan so I just winged things until it was obvious that I needed to move back home. Once I saved up and was ready the second time around, I made a list of my expenses and included cushion for emergencies. The list also included expenses for clothing, eating out and going to the movies. Make it realistic so you can see where you need to cut back, save, and not put yourself in the hole each month. Living on your own may mean hanging out and eating out less. You will have to sacrifice.

You cannot live on your own unless you have a job. Depending on the area, you may need two jobs to live comfortably. A landlord will not rent their place to you if you do not have a steady income. Since you are starting out, many will require an established person to co-sign the apartment in case you fail to pay the rent. In most cases, it is a good idea to have a roommate to split all of the living costs equally. Count up the costs before you venture out on your own. Talk to others who have done it and listen to their advice and learn from their mistakes. If you are not mature and responsible in handling money, you will not live on your own for long.

SUCCESS

"If I was going to be successful,
I had to be successful with myself.
I couldn't be successful doing
what other people were doing...
The worst thing to be is as
successful as someone else.
That's a very difficult thing
to upkeep and very tiring."
— Jay Z

Money is important and has a place in your life. However, there is a big disconnect with believing that money equals success. Success is personal. It is a self-defined term that only matters to you. Money can't buy success or happiness. We live in such a materialistic society that judges us based on our income or the things we have. Do your own research. You will be surprised at the number of rich "successful" people who led depressed, unhappy lives. Just look at some of the struggles rich celebrities face today. Having more money than you could ever spend, will likely lead to drama and problems.

"I don't know what they want from me
It's like the more money we come across
The more problems we see..."
— Mo Money, Mo Problems,
The Notorious B.I.G.

Your definition of success may be finishing college and then traveling the world to help fight against hunger. Although you may not make a lot of money, helping one family or village at a time will be a success for you. Giving of yourself to others may make you happier than you ever imagined. Being committed and having a passion for something you desire, and ultimately achieving that goal, is success.

As you mature, you will realize that having a loving family that you can take care of is in fact success. Each day that you are given the opportunity to be on Earth, you will see that your most valuable asset is your health. Having a healthy body and sound mind outweighs money. There are so many great men who literally changed the world, yet are gone too soon, as their money could not buy their health. Every time you pick up your iPhone, think of the enormous contribution the late, great Steve Jobs made to the world. In addition, we lost the first African-American billionaire, Reginald F. Lewis, to illness in the prime of his career. Regardless of all his accolades and money, the most important thing to him was seeing his son graduate from high school.

UNLEASHING THE KING INSIDE

Knowing how to handle money is a big responsibility and if you make an effort to learn the basics, it will help you in other areas of life. Managing your money wisely is a sign of maturity that will also help build your character and reputation. Dream big and work hard to achieve your goals. Put money in its rightful place as a tool to live. Don't chase money, yet put yourself in a position where opportunities will chase you. Man up and be accountable for your finances to unleash **The King Inside**.

Next Steps: Taking King Initiatives

- Don't give in to every urge to buy something because "it's your own money!" Put yourself on a budget to plan your spending.

- Try to cut back on expenses. Every other weekend, rent movies with friends instead of going to the theater every week. Take turns with your friends buying the latest video games.

- Be careful about providing your personal information online and to others. Identity theft is a major issue, and if your identity is hacked, it may take a long time to clean up your credit record.

- Don't rush into getting credit cards. You will have plenty of time to accumulate debt! If you fail to pay your credit card debt, your employer can garnish your wages.

- Develop good spending habits with the money you earn now.

App #8

Business Foundation

"Greatness is not this wonderful, esoteric, elusive, God-like, feature that only the special among us will ever taste. It's something that truly exists in all of us. It's very simple. This is what I believe, and I'm willing to die for it."

— Will Smith

t is a great idea to learn about business at a young age. Business is happening all around you. You may not think of cutting grass, shoveling snow, washing cars, or trading sneakers or clothing as a business, but your interactions with others in the buying and selling of your services or trading products, are in fact conducting business.

Every day you are engaging in business when you are a paying customer of an organization. Of course, the companies you are likely doing business with are large corporations. However, chances are, these companies started off very small, and many leaders of these large corporations, probably ran several small businesses before they became successful.

> **BUSINESS:** the practice of making a living buying and selling a product or service. An **entrepreneur** is a risk-taking business owner who undertakes an innovative venture to bring the next best product or service to the global marketplace.

Owning a business is hard work. It takes a special amount of passion, dedication and determination to be successful. If business ownership is something you have thought about, do your research on the industry and your target market, while trying to get some experience in the field. There are tons of business resources available from the Small Business Administration and other organizations. The government encourages business ownership as it helps stimulate the economy with job creation. Go for it!

One of the biggest advantages you have in starting a business is the fact that you are technologically savvy. That means you know how to use the latest technology and are very quick learners. All of the new apps and other internet tools have made doing business around the world a lot faster and easier. Being your own boss can be a lot cooler than being an employee, but remember that since you are starting out, you have to be flexible enough to wear a lot of hats; sales, advertising and marketing, website, customer service, and bookkeeping.

Download this

You're never too young to start a business. There is no age limit for a great idea for a new product or service. Oftentimes, younger people are better positioned to see a need in the market, since you are more in tune with your peers and technology.

Are You A Good Fit?

The idea of being your own boss sounds great. You have no one to answer to or any worries about being fired. It's a huge responsibility. Can you handle it?

It takes a certain type of person to be at their best when no one is looking over their shoulder to clock in or out. As I mentioned earlier, you have to wear several hats every day and become good at a lot of things quickly.

One of the most challenging things for people is time management. How good are you at managing your time now? Are your assignments on time? Do you arrive early for work? Are family and friends constantly waiting for you to show up? Are you a procrastinator? If you have not exercised good time management habits, then starting your own business may not be right for you now. It takes practice and is a learned process.

Another key personality trait that you need as a business owner is that you have to be a genuine go-getter. Customers are not just going to find you. You have to go out and get them. In addition, you have to know your market and be skilled enough to anticipate their needs and plan ahead. If you are going to succeed, you have to be self-motivated and prepared for the highs and lows with owning a business.

The key is to have a solid written business plan with realistic projections so you can withstand the ups and downs, and be able to revise the plan as needed. You will also need a detailed marketing plan to hone in on your target market. Most people want to skip the written plans because the idea is so great and customers are asking for the product or service. If you are serious about starting a business, be prepared for uncertainty. Your plan should have alternative strategies during challenging times and thoughts of quitting.

INVESTING

Stocks & Bonds

Our economy is built on business growth. As touched upon earlier, both the state and federal government encourage small business ownership. Just like you are never too young to start a business, you are not too young to learn the basics of investing and how the stock market works. There are tons of resources to provide you with information, so please talk to your mentor or other advisor and do your research.

Keep in mind that investing is a risky business. The stock market will always be unpredictable. You could make a profit or you could lose a lot of money. Stocks tend to be more risky than bonds because they are relying on a corporation meeting or exceeding its projections. As with anything, no matter how much research and past history, unexpected things could go wrong. Bonds are less risky because they are usually backed (guaranteed) by the government and stable banks. They have a lower rate of return.

Many young people can get started in the market by using a technique called Dollar Cost Averaging (DCA). Using the DCA method you can buy a stock of a company for a set dollar amount regardless of the share price. This means you can buy more stock when the price is low and less when the price is high. Either way, you can set up bi-weekly or monthly purchase amounts for a company you believe in.

If there are companies that you are interested in purchasing shares, the first thing to do is to get a copy of their investors' package which should be available online. Keep in mind that there are fees for investing and fees to make transactions. Choose companies that you are familiar with and are already a purchaser of their product or service. You can track your stocks on your phone with various apps.

UNLEASHING THE KING INSIDE

Great ideas come and go. It doesn't matter how old you are. The key is committing the time to put your thoughts on paper, forming a good team, and starting your business venture with the help of mentors and other business experts. There are hundreds of successful young people running businesses all around the country. Put on your business owner's hat and unleash **The King Inside**.

Next Steps: Taking King Initiatives

- Think of things that you are good at and enjoy doing. Find a niche in that thing which may become a business venture. Is there something that you go to reach for or do and you realize there isn't an app or way to do it?

- Don't take your education for granted. Foundational academic skills are fundamental in business.

- If your school offers economics or other business classes make sure you register for them.

- Read books on finances to learn how to save and invest.

- Read books on successful entrepreneurs to witness their challenges and then ultimate rise to success.

App #9

Female Foundation

*"She is a friend of mind. She gather me, man.
The pieces I am, she gather them and give
them back to me in all the right order.
It's good, you know, when you got
a woman who is a friend of your mind."*

— *Beloved, Toni Morrison*

If you haven't experienced it by now, everyone has an opinion about relationships. Especially yours! There are millions of books to tell you how to behave from a psychological standpoint to personal self-help. You've probably received advice from your mom, grandma, auntie, dad, uncles, and of course your friends. No matter what anyone says, always know that no one is an expert in this area, even if their title is "Relationship Expert." Relationships are complicated, emotional experiences that help us mature and learn more about ourselves. They can be challenging because no two people are exactly alike, so your interactions can be great, or ones that you try to forget.

We are all visual beings by nature. So naturally, you are attracted to a female based on her looks. Yet looks fade, or she may be beautiful on the outside, yet extremely unattractive on the inside. Therefore, try not to go for looks alone. Seek females who are smart, kind, and have educational-inspired plans for the future. Like the lines above from the classic book, **Beloved**, look for a female that will be your best friend and has a great mind.

Also, keep your radar up for red flags from females that signal jealousy, high maintenance, extreme desire to be seen, bossy, insecurity: "I'm nothing without you," gossiper, and ones that are dead set on changing you. Over time, you will find yourself in arguments frequent confrontations that may be emotionally draining.

The other side of the coin is that you need to have something to offer a female who has her head on straight. Besides having a strong family, and an educational and spiritual foundation, you must also have a strong moral code. That internal code is one that respects females and does not tolerate nor take part in violence against them, no matter what the circumstances. One slip up can cost you your future. It is unfortunate, but many of you have not had strong male role models to teach you how to treat females.

Check Yourself

When getting into relationships, it's a good idea to have specific standards and qualities that you desire in a female. Yet all too often you get focused on the list of what you want, but fail to take an honest look at yourself to see if *you* are in fact ready. Relationships require time to develop. Do you have the time to invest in building one? Have you completed some of your short-term or long-term goals? Do you have a steady job?

As you may have seen by now, when you rush into

a relationship without having a serious mindset or plans for your future, it is easy to become distracted, and turn your focus to your new love interest. The more you put off doing things to better yourself, the harder it will be to complete them in the long run.

Take time to revisit the chapters on spirituality and self-empowerment. You should really be in tune with yourself before you engage in a serious relationship with someone else. Seek female friends to hang out with on the weekends, but during the week, you should be hard at work on achieving your goals.

Compatibility

Most relationships start out exciting and fun. However, once the newness wears off, you really need to consider if you are going to be in the relationship for the long haul. That is when you should start asking yourself whether you are really compatible with the person.

Now that you have gotten to know her a little better, is she striving to achieve her career goals? How do her goals fit into your plans? Have you discussed it? Is she always late and you are always early? Is she neat and you are messy? Does she have habits that get on your nerves? Is she a spender while you are saving for a rainy day? Are you a sports fanatic and she never watches or participated in sports?

Knowing the answers to these types of questions and more, will help you determine your compatibility. No two people are 100% compatible, however, the two of you should have a few things in common that create a bond, while keeping the moments special and conversation flowing.

What a Girl Wants...

Every girl wants to feel special. Sometimes, your girl wants you to pay attention to her like there is no one else in the room. If you haven't figured it out by now, females can be more emotional than males. We are internally designed differently than you. With that said, females need more honest and open communication regularly. If you are serious with a female, let her know early on of your future plans for the relationship. This will help both of you to be clear about the future.

There can never be an all-inclusive list that applies to every female, but there will always be concepts and steps that most females have in common. Here's my short list:

✓ Girls want to feel protected.

✓ Girls want honest guys.

✓ Girls want guys who are intelligent.

✓ Girls want guys with a sense of humor.

✓ Girls want guys who are good listeners.

✓ Girls want guys with good manners.

✓ Girls want guys to remember their birthdays and special occasions.

✓ Girls want guys who look good in their clothes.

What Girls Don't Want...

✓ Girls don't want guys who cheat.

✓ Girls don't want guys with lots of single friends.

✓ Girls don't want guys who brag all the time.

✓ Girls don't want guys who procrastinate.

✓ Girls don't want cheap guys.

✓ Girls don't want guys with personal hygiene challenges.

Let's Talk About Sex ...

I know you probably think you know all there is to know about sex. Like your generation and others, those who have already experienced it, think they have mastered the subject. Again, relationships are complicated, and having sex at a young age, makes things even more complicated. My parents advised my siblings and myself on the benefits of abstinence. Back then, sex was not as open and visual as it is today. There will be plenty of time for sex and there will be girls eager to engage in the act as well.

"Hate to sound sleazy,

but tease me,

I don't want it, if it's that easy..."

— I Get Around, Tupac Shakur

Every decision you make in life has consequences. Having sex is no different. Trust me, I know it is difficult to have discipline in this area. As a teacher, I overhear sex-related conversations daily. Many of my students have become fathers at young ages. Now, they have to focus on finishing their studies and taking care of a child.

Fatherhood

Young people having sex is nothing new, yet at the end of the day, mental readiness and physical readiness are two different things. If you are a young father, your child's birth is not an accident or mistake. Regardless of the circumstances, everything happens for a reason, and you were put into that child's life for a specific purpose. Own up to your responsibilities as a father. Having a child is not the end of the world. It is the beginning of your maturity into manhood. Now, you should be even more focused on achieving your goals. Seek advice and help from those you respect and research organizations to assist you in balancing your new life as a student, father, athlete, and employee. It will be challenging, but it can be done with the right attitude and determination to succeed. If your relationship with the child's mother is over, don't let that ruin your relationship with your child.

King's Wisdom...

""I was a high school senior being recruited by Division I colleges in two sports: football and basketball. I just found out that I had a baby girl. I kept repeating to myself, *It's not over. You just made it harder for yourself.* I reasoned."
Excerpt from Playing Up: One's Man Rise From Public Housing to Public Service Through Mentorship."

—Vaughn L. McKoy, JD, MBA

UNLEASHING THE KING INSIDE

Relationships take time. Don't rush into new relationships, as you have plenty of time to grow as a person, before you devote time and energy into "fixing" someone else. Hang out with females who are headed in a path that you admire. Stay focused on your goals and vision for you future, without getting wrapped up into someone else's dream. At this point in your life, the more you focus on bettering yourself, without additional female distractions, the more likely you will achieve your goals and unleash **The King Inside**.

Next Steps: Taking King Initiatives

- We are all complicated human beings. Pay attention to the warning signs and do not stay with someone because of her physical appearance.

- It's not good to get involved with someone who is jealous. This is a sign of insecurity and low self-esteem, which may cause problems.

- Don't lose yourself to please someone else. Make time to hang out with your friends and family.

- Be clear on what you are seeking in a relationship and if the person does not have the qualities or mindset that are important to you, stop wasting both of your time.

- Above all else, beware of TRAPS!

App #10

Pay-It-Forward Foundation

"Life's most persistent and urgent question is, 'what are you doing for others?'".

— *Dr. Martin Luther King Jr.*

Helping others is should be one of the most important character traits you possess. We were designed to use our gifts and talents to benefit others as well as ourselves. Life has a reciprocal principle—you get what you put out. Therefore, if you shift your mindset from selfishness and a "what's in it for me?" attitude, then more opportunities will arise for you.

A good way to get involved in paying it forward is to volunteer in your community. There are so many causes for you to be inspired to help. Find something that you are passionate about like a healthier community, safety, after-school programs (activities and academics), teen support groups, anti-bullying, the elderly and the environment are just a few examples.

Volunteering gives you a chance to share your skills with others, as well as practice your communication, organization, and leadership skills. You may be fortunate and learn a new area of community service or business. All of the roles and responsibilities you perform while volunteering can be highlighted on your resume and college applications.

The satisfaction that you feel when you lend a hand to help others cannot be monetized. As you further your career, you will see the benefit of reaching back as a mentor, event organizer or donor. There are so many athletes, celebrities, and leaders, who donate their time and money throughout the year for causes they believe in. Even though you may just be starting out, your efforts are just as valuable as someone more experienced and well-known.

I've found that it can be difficult for young people to envision helping others because they may not have experienced anyone helping them. That's why it is important to step outside of your comfort zone, see how others are living, in order to help shape your views about your future, and what you have to offer.

Exposure

In my experience, there is a necessary mindset shift that has to occur for you to see yourself beyond your neighborhood. I started my education career as a high school teacher in Camden, New Jersey. Although I was the instructor, I learned more from my students than I ever imagined. One day, our lesson involved dreams and visions for the future. I can still recall it today. The title was "Dream Big, The Possibilities Are Endless." As part of the activity, the students were asked to write and/or draw their dream home and ideal careers. I gave vivid examples which included illustrations on the board. To my surprise, many drew one and two bedroom apartments and surprisingly small condos. When I advised them to dream bigger than an apartment, the looks on their faces were like a deer in headlights. I said, "What about grass? Don't you want grass, flowers or trees?" None of them desired anything from nature. Don't get me wrong, of course you can live in cities with high-end apartments without a lawn or flowers.

Then, the conversation turned to cars. Many students were astonished that I drove a luxury SUV and was not a drug dealer. Many of them had cars parked directly in front of their apartments. I asked, "If everyone has a car, where is your garage? Don't you want a garage?" None of them thought a garage was a big deal. Throughout our discussions, the students were excited and engaged in their drawings and narratives, literally walking around to see and hear what their peers had drawn. One group was talking about laundry. I chimed in, "So where is your laundry room in your apartment?" The response from one of my male students gave me more pause than the lack of a front lawn. "Ms. Rouse, I don't need a laundry room. My apartment is only one block from the laundromat!" Other students agreed.

"So Ms. Rouse, do you have a laundry room?"
"Yes, as a matter of fact I do."
"So where do you live?"
"In Burlington."

"Burlington? Where's that?"

"Don't tell me you have never heard of Burlington! It's only 17 miles from here!"

I must admit, I was startled that in a room of 12 students, not one of them had explored past 20 miles beyond their neighborhood, off a main route between my house and their school. I immediately went to the administration and filled out a trip request form to drive them to other neighborhoods not farther than my home. They were awestruck when we explored nearby neighborhoods. Of course I have read about and agreed with the lack of exposure component for youth self-empowerment, but to experience it first-hand was eye-opening.

There is no doubt that African-Americans and Latinos have large purchasing power, cultural influence, and talent, however, these two minority groups still make up a small amount of the total U.S. population. The challenge is that in your neighborhoods, you are surrounded by people who look like you, act like you, and for the most part, may think like you. This can have both positive and negative effects. You must realize that *your* limited view of the world is just that— limited. So many people are living differently, thinking differently, and dreaming bigger. If everyone around you is doing things that are non-productive or destructive to themselves and the community, every now and then, ride a bus, a train, or get a ride from someone with a car, to expose yourself to different environments. In order to broaden your vision, you must picture yourself beyond the block.

Download this

*As of 2014, according to the U.S. Census, individuals of White descent comprise about **77%** of the U.S. population, Black or African descent comprise about **14%**, and Hispanics and Latinos are **17.4%**. Think about these numbers. Your block or your crew is only a glimpse of what the U.S. and the world looks like as a whole. Get off your block often to expose your mind to other possibilities.*

King's Wisdom...

"In many of our communities people are only concerned with themselves; "self-preservation." I would contribute this to the social economic structure of our country. Because of the societal pressures, those who find themselves living day-to-day or month-to-month, are so consumed with accomplishing short term activities that they do not have time to see long term solutions to simple issues. Education is paramount in the process of being a "good citizen."

—Keith Watson, Memphis, TN

UNLEASHING THE KING INSIDE

Having a sense of social responsibility to others in your community is a sign of maturity. By taking the focus off yourself, you are positioning your future for a positive outcome. The benefits of volunteering your time cannot be measured in dollars. Your satisfaction in knowing your efforts made a difference in an organization or an individual's situation is fulfilling, and will energize you to do more. Commit to making a personal investment to better the lives of others to unleash **The King Inside.**

Next Steps: Taking Kingship Initiatives

- Think about the things you are passionate about. Was there an area in your life where you felt neglected? Volunteering for causes that hit home is the start of paying it forward.

- Research your favorite celebrities, athletes, and business leaders to see what causes are important to them. Many famous people have their own organizations or are part of national and international causes that may also be of interest to you.

- Increase your awareness of what is going on in your community and around the world.

- Network with those at different levels in their career whom you share similar interests, as volunteer opportunities may arise out of your association.

- Research the established black fraternities. Joining a fraternity is a great way to enhance your leadership skills and work alongside peers who have worked in several communities for various causes.

Final Thoughts...

"If people are informed they will do the right thing. It's when they are not informed that they become hostages to prejudice."

- Charlayne Hunter-Gault

Your communities need you to be leaders. They need positive forces to bring about change. As I write this final chapter, the world has recently witnessed graphic video footage of the murders of two Black men at the hands of white police officers in two different states; Alton Sterling, in Baton Rouge, Louisiana and Philando Castile, in St. Paul Minnesota. These back-to-back killings are devastating, to say the least. Watching the inhuman shooting of these young men sent chills down my spine. It could have been one of my sons, nephews, cousins or other relatives! To watch young men being murdered at the hands of police officers is utterly horrific.

Unfortunately, as an African-American male, you are automatically presumed a criminal in the eyes of some law enforcement officers around the country. These recent deaths are positive examples of using modern technology along with social media for a good cause. Yet it depicts a clear and chilling message that it doesn't matter whether you comply with a police officer's request or respond in an unthreatening manner, there are police officers who view their badges as a justifiable right to "shoot to kill." This disproportionate, negative perception of young Black men has to change. You are kings, leaders, husbands, fathers, sons, friends, and so much more.

Change must come from our federal and state politicians, our community leaders, athletes, celebrities, corporate leaders, and generations of people of all races and cultures. However, we cannot make change by answering violence with more violence. Such action is never the solution. The same mentality that says all Black males are criminals is the same short-sighted view which says all police officers are bad. There are many decent police officers in this country who deserve our praise and highest esteem. Let's face it, there are Black and white male criminals and there are corrupted Black and white police officers. But that should not stop us from doing what is right.

We must stand together and demand that justice is served on those police officers who murder African-American men in cold blood under the pretense of their perceived threat of danger. Such officers must be held accountable to the fullest extent of the law. You can make a difference by using challenging racial incidents like these to unleash The King Inside.

"...with liberty and justice for all."

—*The Pledge of Allegiance,*
The United States of America

Bonus King's Wisdom

There is more wisdom from men who have been in your shoes that you can learn from to help you along your journey. Take the time to read them and hopefully these words will connect with you.

"You have enormous potential and you should work every day to realize the full extent of that potential. Commit to making a positive impact on your community. There is no greater praise that someone can give you than to say that they are better off for you having come their way. Strive to have that impact on all that you meet."

— Hon. Troy Singleton
Assemblyman 7th District NJ

A person has to remember that the road to success is always under construction. You have to get that through your head. That it is not easy becoming successful."

— *Steve Harvey*

"Everything negative — pressure, challenges — is all an opportunity for me to rise."

— *Kobe Bryant*

"There can be no healthy relationship of any sort without respect. If respect is there, everything else will fall in place. Respect is willing to listen to other people's ideas, even if you have decided that you are going with your own. Respect is talking to people in a tone of voice that is not demeaning. And respect is treating others the way that you want to be treated."

— George Stewart III,
Educator/Youth Program Developer

"Too many of us are looking for our moment on the bus, when we should be spending more time behind the scenes strategizing how to eliminate the real "vehicle" blocking our progress toward justice."

— *Marcus "Goodie" Goodloe, Ph.D.*

"My goal is to build a life I don't need a vacation from."

— *Rob Hill Sr.*

Extra Bonus Queen's Wisdom

Wisdom comes from different influences. This book is filled with wisdom from men that have experienced life's challenges and succeeded. However, it is worthy to mention that many African-American women have had the immense task of furthering their education, pursuing a career and single-handedly raise a family. Whether impactful advice comes from a male or female, it is bound to have a positive impact on your future. Take note of some of the empowering quotes from many outstanding women trailblazers of recent years.

"When you walk with purpose, you collide with destiny."

— Bertice Berry

"If you don't like something, change it. If you can't change it, change your attitude."

— *Maya Angelou*

"Don't wait around for other people to be happy for you. Any happiness you get you've got to make yourself."

— *Alice Walker*

"Living in the moment means letting go of the past and not waiting for the future. It means living your life consciously, aware that each moment you breathe is a gift."

— *Oprah Winfrey*

"Deal with yourself as an individual worthy of respect, and make everyone else deal with you the same way. "

— *Nikki Giovanni*

"Whatever is bringing you down, get rid of it. Because you'll find that when you're free . . . your true self comes out."

— *Tina Turner*

"Take responsibility for yourself because no one's going to take responsibility for you. I'm not a victim. I grow from this and I learn."

— *Tyra Banks*

"The times may have changed, but the people are still the same. We're still looking for love, and that will always be our struggle as human beings."

— *Halle Berry*

"It's time for you to move, realizing that the thing you are seeking is also seeking you."

— *Iyanla Vanzant*

"'I can't' are two words that have never been in my vocabulary. I believe in me more than anything in this world."

— *Wilma Rudolph*

"Fear is a disease that eats away at logic and makes man inhuman."

— *Marian Anderson*

About the Author

Dr. Angelise M. Rouse is an education writer and staunch special education advocate. Her interest focus is on creating a meaningful, lasting and empowering educational experience for students with disabilities. Her research examines the development of opportunities to learn in special education classrooms, and how these opportunities are negotiated differently by various groups of students.

Inspired by her doctoral dissertation topic, Dr. Rouse future research interests are in the overrepresentation of minorities in special education and the emotional development of African-American young males. Dr. Rouse holds several educational certifications and has been thoroughly published on critical educational issues. She has worked in several educational arenas serving as a charter and public school teacher, school administrator and college faculty member. Her work ranges from all levels of education from middle school through college.

Dr. Rouse holds a Ph.D. in Special Education Leadership and received a Masters in Organizational Management and Special Education. Her first book, Especially 4 Me: A Student's Guide to Understanding the IEP, was written to help promote self-advocacy for special education students. Her latest publication, **The King Inside: A Practical Guide for Young African-American Males**, was written to encourage and motivate young African-American Males to succeed and navigate life's challenges into adulthood. She is currently working on her next publication which will highlight urban education and inner city matters, specifically as they relate to educational research, policy, and practice.

Dr. Rouse believes everyone has captivating stories to tell and each story is as unique and individual as the strands on our heads. She believes that our personal insight gives substance and credence to our experiences and ideas to bring forth change. It's time more educators position ourselves to make positive changes to educating all students on new levels.

References

Bastani, Janice. *Eve: Reclaim Your Power!*
Pleasanton, CA: Counts, 2013. Print.

"Black Boys Report." Schott Foundation for Public
Education. N.p., n.d. Web. 15 June 2016.

Black Fraternities and Sororities: The Divine Nine.
(n.d.). Retrieved May 2, 2016, from http://www.cam-
pusexplorer.com/college-advice-tips/851FB5B7/
Black-Fraternities-and-Sororities-The-Divine-Nine

Familylife.(n.d.). Retrieved April 13, 2016,
from http://www.familylife.com/articles/topics/
life-issues/relationships/honoring-your-parents

Kafele, B. K. (2009). Motivating Black Males To
Achieve In School & In Life. Alexandria, VA: ASCD.

Kunjufu, J. (2011). Understanding Black Male Learning Styles. Chicago, IL: African American Images.

LiveboldandBloom. Retrieved May 13, 2016 from:// liveboldandbloom.com/01/life-coaching/the-secret-life-of-the-self-empowered

Population Estimates, July 1, 2015, (V2015)." *UNITED STATES QuickFacts from the US Census Bureau.* N.p., n.d. Web. 17 June 2016.

Self-Empowered-The Secret Life. (2012). Retrieved May 12, 2016, from http://liveboldandbloom. com/01/life-coaching/the-secret-life-of-the-self-empowered

"The Importance of Positive Male Role Models." *First Things First*. N.p., 22 Sept. 2015. Web. 16 June 2016.

Thompson, G. L. (2004). Through Ebony Eyes: What teachers Need To Know But Are Afraid To Ask About African-American Students. San Francisco, CA: Jossey-Bass.

Why Every School in America Should Teach Entrepreneurship | TIME.com. (n.d.). Retrieved June 12, 2016, fromhttp://business.time.com/2012/06/01/why-every-school-in-america-should-teach-entrepreneurship/

Resources[2]

Below are additional resources for you to research many of the topics discussed to give you a stronger foundation as you apply them to your goals. There are many other resources out there so take the initiative to do your part to move forward. Think about what options you have as you learn to explore new possibilities.

Education

The College Board: www.collegeboard.org
The College Navigator: www.nces.ed.gov
Cappex: www.cappex.com
College Majors: www.collegemajors101.com
College Insight: www.college-insight.org
College Results: www.collegeresults.org

Mentorship

My Brothers Keeper: www.whitehouse.gov/my-brothers-keepers

---

2. The information provided in this Resources section is for informational purposes only. Especially 4 Me Publishing LLC does not endorse nor accept responsibility for the content or accuracy of the website information.

Men's Empowerment Network: www.men-intl.com
100 Black Men: www.100blakmen.org
Mentoring USA: www.mentorihgusa.org
Big Brothers Big Sisters of America: www.bbbs.org
Mentoring to Manhood: www.mentoring2manhood.
org
Mentoring Male Teens: www.mentoringmaleteens.
org

Self-Empowerment

Boys and Girls Club of America: www.bgca.org
Empowering Black Men and Boys to Transform
Their Communities: www.okprogram.org
Campaign for Black Male Achievement: www.black-
maleachievement.org

Money

The US Mint: www.themint.org
Balance Track: www.balancetrack.org
Warren Buffett Advice: http://www.cnbc.
com/2013/11/22/buffett-how-to-teach-your-your-
kids-about-moneycommentary.html

Teen Entrepreneurs

http://www.teenbusiness.com/
http://www.inc.com/ss/6-richest-teen-entrepre-
neurs
http://www.cnn.com/2014/12/08/business/teen-en-
trepreneurs-making-millions/

https://www.entrepreneur.com/topic/kids

Business Plans: SBA.gov

Pay It Forward

Volunteering: www.volunteermatch.org

Do Something: www.dosomething.org/us

*"Change will not come if we wait
for some other person or some other time.
We are the ones we've been waiting for.
We are the change that we seek."*

— President Barack Obama

FOR MORE INFORMATION LOG ON TO

www.especially4mepublishing.com

Made in United States
Troutdale, OR
04/26/2024

19462032R00086